Put Beginning Readers on the Right Track with
ALL ABOARD READING™

The All Aboard Reading series is especially designed for beginning readers. Written by noted authors and illustrated in full color, these are books that children really want to read—books to excite their imagination, expand their interests, make them laugh, and support their feelings. With fiction and nonfiction stories that are high interest and curriculum-related, All Aboard Reading books offer something for every young reader. And with four different reading levels, the All Aboard Reading series lets you choose which books are most appropriate for your children and their growing abilities.

Picture Readers
Picture Readers have super-simple texts, with many nouns appearing as rebus pictures. At the end of each book are 24 flash cards—on one side is a rebus picture; on the other side is the written-out word.

Station Stop 1
Station Stop 1 books are best for children who have just begun to read. Simple words and big type make these early reading experiences more comfortable. Picture clues help children to figure out the words on the page. Lots of repetition throughout the text helps children to predict the next word or phrase—an essential step in developing word recognition.

Station Stop 2
Station Stop 2 books are written specifically for children who are reading with help. Short sentences make it easier for early readers to understand what they are reading. Simple plots and simple dialogue help children with reading comprehension.

Station Stop 3
Station Stop 3 books are perfect for children who are reading alone. With longer text and harder words, these books appeal to children who have mastered basic reading skills. More complex stories captivate children who are ready for more challenging books.

In addition to All Aboard Reading books, look for All Aboard Math Readers™ (fiction stories that teach math concepts children are learning in school) and All Aboard Science Readers™ (nonfiction books that explore the most fascinating science topics in age-appropriate language).

All Aboard for happy reading!

For my Pop-Pop, in loving memory—J.H.

In memory of Emilio and Carmelina
González Trujillo—P.J.G.

Library of Congress Cataloging-in-Publication Data

Huelin, Jodi.
    Turtles / by Jodi Huelin ; illustrated by Pedro Julio Gonzalez.
      p .cm. — (All aboard science reader. Station stop 1)
      Summary: Desribes the anatomy, behavior, and life cycle of land and sea turtles.
    1. Turtles—Juvenile literature. [1. Turtles.] I. Gonzalez, Pedro Julio, ill. II. Title.
    III. Series: All aboard science reader. Station stop 1.
    QL666.C5 H84 2003
    597.92—dc21

                                                                            2002151239

ISBN 0-448-43117-3 (pbk)   A B C D E F G H I J
ISBN 0-448-43143-2 (GB)   A B C D E F G H I J

All Aboard Science Reader™

Turtles

By Jodi Huelin
Illustrated by Pedro Julio González

Grosset & Dunlap • New York

Look over there—

in the water.

Do you see a turtle?

LOGGERHEAD TURTLE

LOGGERHEAD TURTLE

It is a sea turtle.

It has long, strong flippers.

They help the turtle to swim.

Sea turtles are
almost always swimming.

This sea turtle
has come on land.
She is ready to lay her eggs!

LOGGERHEAD TURTLE

She lays her eggs at night.

She lays them in holes.

Then she goes back to the water.

9

Two months pass.

The eggs hatch one by one.

After three days,

the baby turtles head

for the water.

GREEN TURTLE
HATCHLINGS

Only a few will make it.
Baby turtles are a tasty snack
for birds and animals.

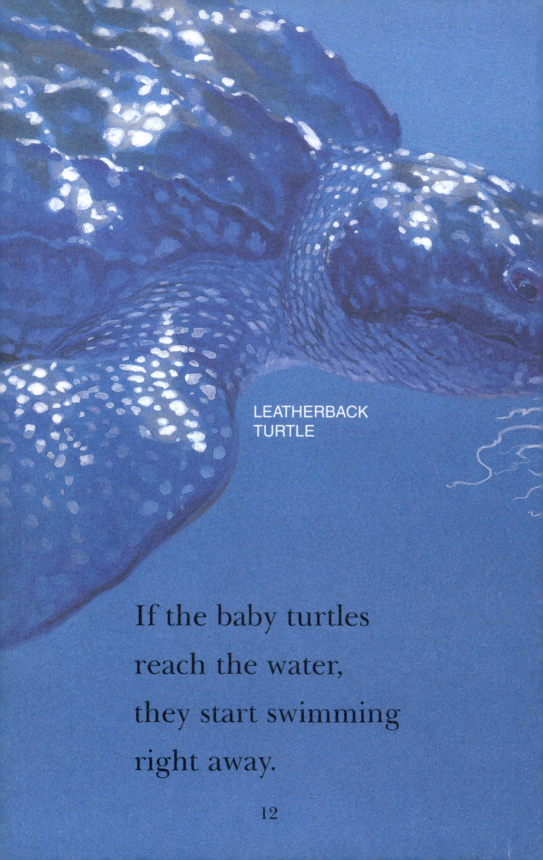

LEATHERBACK
TURTLE

If the baby turtles
reach the water,
they start swimming
right away.

Sea turtles are good swimmers.
Sea turtles are good divers, too.
Some like to dive for jellyfish.

Different sea turtles
eat different things.
Some eat plants.
Like sea grass and seaweed.

GREEN TURTLE

OLIVE RIDLEY

Others eat small creatures.
Like clams and shrimp.

EAST RIVER
COOTER

Turtles need soft food—
they don't have teeth!
They do have <u>very</u> strong jaws.

16

Turtles also have beaks.

The beaks help them tear food.

Even though turtles

don't have teeth,

they can still bite.

SNAPPING TURTLE

BOX TURTLE

Some turtles live on land.

They are usually called tortoises.

18

They do not swim.
They only go to water
to drink and take a bath.

19

You can visit turtles at the zoo.

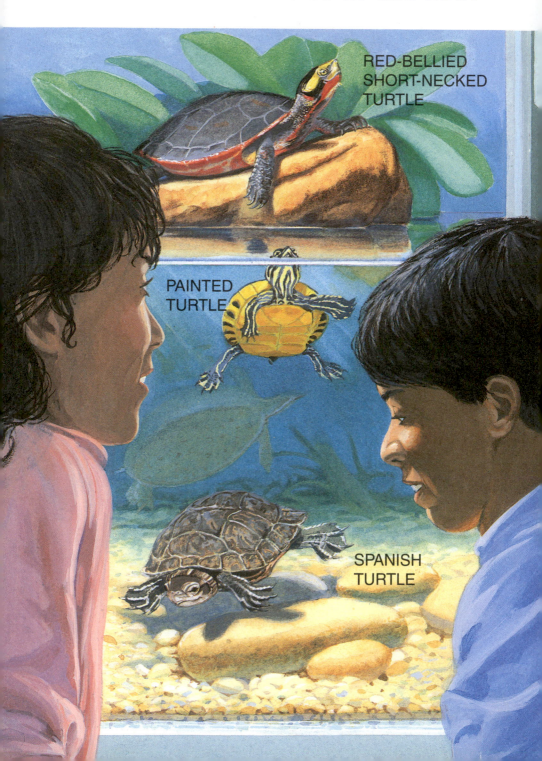

RED-BELLIED
SHORT-NECKED
TURTLE

PAINTED
TURTLE

SPANISH
TURTLE

You can keep some kinds
of turtles as pets.

BABY
PAINTED
TURTLE

Always wash your hands
after you touch a turtle.

Sea turtles and land turtles
can live indoors in a fish tank.
Land turtles can also live
outside in a pen.

TORTOISE

You can feed them salad
and flowers and fruits
and vegetables.

Some turtles live
a pretty long time.
Like 30 or 40 years.

PAINTED TURTLE

Other turtles live
a <u>really</u> long time.
Like 70 or 80 years.

GIANT
GALAPAGOS
TORTOISE

CAR

LEATHERBACK TURTLE

BOG TURTLE

Some turtles are
a few inches long.

LEATHERBACK TURTLE

BOG TURTLE

But some are over six feet long.

That's almost as long as a car!

DESERT TORTOISE

Most turtles have soft bodies
and hard shells.
The shell protects the turtle.
It keeps the turtle's body safe.

Land turtles can tuck
their head and legs
in their shell
if there is danger.
Sea turtles can't do this.

DESERT TORTOISE

GREEN TURTLE

So what do sea turtles do
if there is danger?
They swim away, of course!